MIKE STEELE

**UNDERSTANDING STORMS IN THE LIFE OF THE BELIEVER**

# WHY, GOD?
UNDERSTANDING STORMS IN THE LIFE OF THE BELIEVER

By Mike Sternad

Published by: Contented Life Publishing

Calvary Chapel Mobile
312 - T Schillinger Rd. S, Mobile, Alabama 36608

Website: www.calvarychapelmobile.com

Email: mikesternad@gmail.com

Copyright © 2019 by Mike Sternad

All rights reserved. No part of this publication may be reproduced, stored in a retrieval system, or transmitted in any form or by any means without the express written consent of Mike Sternad.

Unless otherwise indicated, Scripture quotations in this book are taken from the New King James Version of the Bible. Copyright © 1979, 1980, 1982 by Thomas Nelson, Inc., Publishers. Used by permission.
Printed in the United States of America

Edited by Miriam Rogers
Cover Design by Ashley Garcia

# TABLE OF CONTENTS

FOREWORD..........5

PREFACE..........6

INTRODUCTION..........7

CHAPTER 1: THE CALM BEFORE THE STORM..........11

CHAPTER 2: THE WIND..........17

CHAPTER 3: THE RAIN..........21

CHAPTER 4: THE DARKNESS..........25

CHAPTER 5: THE STORM..........29

CHAPTER 6: THE CLOUDS..........35

CONCLUSION..........41

ABOUT THE AUTHOR..........44

# FOREWORD

I love reading parables. Parables are defined as "earthly stories with a heavenly meaning." The book you hold in your hands contains many parables that deal with the different types of storms we all experience in life. By giving heavenly meaning to the struggles we face, Mike's words help us survive the harshest storms that may come our way.

I have had the privilege of knowing Mike for many years. I first met him while he was a student at the School of Ministry at Calvary Chapel Costa Mesa. He was, without a doubt, one of my favorite students. After graduating in 2011, he and I continued to stay in touch. Once the Lord put it on his heart to plant a church in Alabama, we would get together to talk about church planting and to pray for the work the Lord had for him there.

There is an old Latin proverb that says "experience is our best teacher." The good news is that we aren't limited to only learning from our own experiences, we may also learn from the experiences of others. In this book you are about to read, Mike does an amazing job of sharing the lessons he has learned through dealing with the storms that have come his way. I learned a great deal and I am positive you will too. Read and receive these parables and you are sure to be blessed.

*Jeff E. Gipe, Pastor and Author*

# PREFACE

I wrote this short book to help you understand that storms are not always setbacks. As a pastor for over a decade, I have seen many believers get sidetracked from the calling God has placed on their lives because of the challenging season or storm they have found themselves in.

Allowing external circumstances to dictate the state of their inward spiritual life, the storms leave them depressed, discouraged or stuck spiritually—unable to move forward. In life, we will all face hard times and stormy seasons. But these storms do not need to draw us away from God's path and calling for us. Even in the midst of storms we can still experience the abundant life that Jesus has promised us.

I hope that while reading this book you will learn not to despise the stormy seasons in life, but rather allow God to work in and through you to build a solid trust in Him. He will never leave you nor forsake you. Storms don't have to stop you in your tracks or steer you away from God's will. You can be sure that although God may have allowed a storm in your life, He will not let you be swept away by the current.

*Mike Sternad*

# INTRODUCTION

Not everyone in Southern California has air conditioning in their home. When we lived in California, our family lived in an apartment close to the beach, and so we had little to no need for air conditioning. During the summer, the cool ocean breeze made its way through our apartment windows, and for the few weeks when the heat was uncomfortable, a pedestal fan in the living room was enough to cool the place down.

When we moved to the Deep South in the summer of 2017, we quickly realized that air conditioning was not a luxury but a necessity. IT. WAS. HOT. The humidity alone caused us instant discomfort. We were constantly dripping in perspiration! During the summer, stores and restaurants ran their air conditioning non-stop to a comfortable sixty-eight degrees.

In Mobile, Alabama, where we now live, it would be scorching hot in the summer mornings and then rain like crazy in the afternoon. Everyone told us about the humidity in the South, but no one mentioned the daily torrential downpours. I remember one time shortly after we first arrived in Mobile, we came outside from shopping at Costco to find what looked like buckets of water pouring out of the heavens. We had never seen that much rain! My wife and I noticed everyone was waiting under the overhang outside of Costco, but we weren't sure why. Being a typical Californian (always in a rush to get everything done), I left my wife with the groceries and ran to pull the car up. By the time I got to the car I was completely soaked. I pulled the car up and my wife got in while I loaded the groceries in the trunk. Almost immediately after we drove away the rain completely stopped. All of the people waiting under the overhang walked to their cars and loaded up their groceries—they were completely dry, while I was soaking wet. My wife and I looked at each other and wondered, "What the heck just happened?" Since then we've become acclimated to the Deep South summer weather patterns; however, we are still in awe of the intense amounts of rain!

Life, like the weather, can be unpredictable. One moment we're enjoying the sunshine and the next we're finding ourselves in the midst of a storm. We see the rain clouds coming or feel the flood waters rising, and we quickly sink in despair. Storms in life have the potential to threaten our spiritual lives and wash away what God has built up within us. God's intent is always that the storms of life would draw us closer to Him, but often we allow the storms to draw us away from Him.

Why do so many believers feel depleted of strength during stormy seasons? Why do so many Christians get discouraged when they go through hard times? I believe this occurs when we look at our external circumstances and allow them to dictate the state of our inward spiritual life. In 2 Corinthians 5:7 Paul wrote, "For we walk by faith, not by sight." Walking by faith means we focus on spiritual matters, the unseen, and we establish our lives upon the Rock, which is Christ (1 Corinthians 10:4).

Walking by faith does not mean we base our lives upon our outward circumstances, the things we can see.

Our natural response in tough times is to pray them away. After all, hard times are evil, right? And yet, all through the Bible God often describes storms as our greatest catalyst for change. Storms don't have to steal our joy or draw us away from God; rather, they can bring us closer to Him. When Jesus is the foundation of our lives, storms may rage around us, but we will not be washed out to sea.

Throughout this book my hope is that you will discover the various types of storms that we believers experience and learn how you can find victory in those difficult seasons.

At the end of each chapter, you will find questions designed to help you better understand what God is doing in your life and how you can be faithful to Him. If you apply these lessons, you will find yourself overcoming storms that you experience over and over again and enjoy a renewed sense of hope and relief.

*"You are of God, little children, and have overcome them, because He who is in you is greater than he who is in the world."* **—1 John 4:4**

CHAPTER 1

# THE
# CALM
# BEFORE
# THE
# STORM

"Therefore whoever hears these sayings of Mine, and does them, I will liken him to a wise man who built his house on the rock: and the rain descended, the floods came, and the winds blew and beat on that house; and it did not fall, for it was founded on the rock."

MATTHEW 7:24-25

AS A YOUNG CHILD I looked forward to my family's annual summer getaway to Half Moon Bay on the coast of California. What I remember most about those trips was the peacefulness of the beach and the joy of being together with my family. I was safe and I was happy. I would lay out on a towel soaking up the sun each day, playing with my family, relaxing and enjoying the view. As an adult, I can imagine why my parents enjoyed taking us there. There's something so majestic and calming about the ocean. The sound of the waves, the coolness of the breeze and the expanse of the ocean can make us forget our worries and fears.

Most of us wish we could experience that type of peace and serenity every day, but life's not like that—not even for people who live on the beaches of California! You may be enjoying a season of calm in your own life right now; the bills are paid, your family is doing well, you are enjoying your job. There is little to stress or worry about. If that's you, this is a season to be thankful for. There's no need to feel guilty that things are going well. It's an amazing experience to find yourself relaxing on the shore of a beautiful beach on a picture-perfect day. These seasons of life are sweet moments where we get to rest and enjoy all that we have and all that we've been given.

As believers, these seasons of external peace and rest are often few and far between. God gives us these moments to pause and reflect on how good He is. He also gives us seasons of external peace to prepare our hearts for the storms of life that inevitably lie ahead.

The calm before the storm is often the time when we can see with the most clarity. Our vision is unobstructed by the clouds or the stormy skies ahead. Just like the ocean on a clear day, we can see God's goodness toward us and enjoy it. We are not caught up in doubt or discouragement or unbelief because we can see clearly.

During these seasons of life, it is important that we use this time of clear vision to focus on Jesus and all that He has done for us. This is a time to grow in gratefulness and praise to God the Father. This season of peace is also a place to learn to rest in God and in His goodness toward you. Enjoy the security that you have found in Christ; He has saved you and has set you apart for His good purposes. He has promised you eternity with Himself. These are moments when we need to lift our hands in praise to God and thank Him for who He is and all that He has done. It is good to be thankful and enjoy these seasons of peace and rest—they are God-given!

As incredible as these seasons of peace and rest are, Jesus warns us not to build our house upon the enjoyment of that sandy beach! Like my family vacations in Half Moon Bay, the summer weather doesn't last forever. If we build our entire foundation around the assumption that the weather will always be clear, or that we'll always be in a season of peace and rest, our *house* won't last.

Jesus doesn't want us to live in fear of our future or to worry about what's coming next during seasons of rest. He wants us to focus on Him and enjoy our present state of peace. But He does want us to build our spiritual house or our foundation of faith in such a way that we can withstand any type of weather or storm.

We build our faith or our spiritual house by planting our lives firmly upon the Rock that is Christ. Even during seasons of rest, we can be establishing ourselves in Christ by placing our faith in Him alone—not in our favorable circumstances, stable finances, happy family, or enjoyable job. Those things may change with the seasons, but Jesus and His love toward us will never fail. He is our shield. He is our fortress. He is our hiding place. No storm can wash away our foundation when our house is built upon the Rock that is Jesus Christ.

# THE CALM BEFORE THE STORM
## QUESTIONS FOR REFLECTION

1. It's important to know we can have peace in both the calm and stormy seasons. Where does our peace come from and how can we obtain this peace?

Read John 14:27 in your Bible to answer this question.

_____

_____

_____

_____

2. What we build our life upon matters. According to these psalms, who is our spiritual foundation? What are you building your life upon?

Read Psalm 62:2 and Psalm 94:22 to answer this question.

_____

_____

_____

_____

## CHAPTER 2

# THE
# WIND

"The wind blows where it wishes, and you hear the sound of it, but cannot tell where it comes from and where it goes. So is everyone who is born of the Spirit."

JOHN 3:8

AS A KID I LOVED flying kites. I enjoyed picking out the kite, tying on the string and letting the wind carry my kite away until the string felt taut in my hands. It was such a thrill, and yet I always had this fear that I'd let go of the kite and it would fly away never to be found again. Even as a child, I knew that the wind was unpredictable. Sometimes within moments the direction of the wind would suddenly change and I'd need to adjust my grip to keep the kite flying up in the air and not crashing to the ground.

Life can seem to be as unpredictable as the wind. We don't always know which direction the wind may blow, and we can't always know what direction our lives may take. As believers, we know God is supernaturally leading our lives, and yet we don't know the full story. Much like my childhood kite flying experiences, when the winds of life change, we need to adjust our grip.

For seasons of wind and change, God gives each one of His children discernment to know how to adjust our grip. Discernment is the ability to understand and know what God is doing in any given situation. We might ask, "Is this merely a slight change in direction, Lord? Or is this a windstorm in which case I may need to pull my kite in and find protection?"

When the winds of change happen, we do not need to be afraid. The storms of life will come and go, but God always stays the same. He is good now and forever. The winds of change do not indicate that God's heart toward you has changed. Externally, you may feel tossed about and confused as to where God is leading you but remember where your help comes from. Psalm 121:2 says, "My help comes from the LORD, the Maker of heaven and earth." He will give you discernment in whatever place you may find yourself this very moment. Seek the Lord and allow Him to bring relief even in the most unfavorable circumstances.

If you are in a season where the wind is blowing and you are uncertain of what God is doing, take heart. God is with you through the constant and the change. Trust Him. He created the wind and He sustains the wind. He created you and He will sustain you. Ask Him for discernment in this season and know that He will safely lead you through it as you trust in Him.

# THE WIND
## QUESTIONS FOR REFLECTION

1. Life can be unpredictable and erratic. How do we remain stable when our circumstances seem so shaky?

Read Hebrews 13:6 and 8 to answer this question.

_____

_____

_____

_____


2. We all face uncertain times. What does Psalm 55:22 tell us we should do with our struggles? What does it say the Lord will do? What promise is there for us?

Read Psalm 55:22 to answer this question.

_____

_____

_____

_____

CHAPTER 3

# THE
# RAIN

"Ask the LORD for rain in the time of the latter rain. The LORD will make flashing clouds; He will give them showers of rain, grass in the field for everyone."

ZECHARIAH 10:1

MY PARENTS HAVE A picture of me as a small child in a bright yellow rain jacket looking upwards, eyes closed and with my mouth open. I grew up in Northern California where we enjoyed more rain than in Southern California. As a child I loved the rain. I'd run out to the streets looking for puddles to jump in and finding new ways to get the biggest splash.

As an adult, I prefer watching the rain from inside where it's dry to running around in it outside. Rain looks less like an adventure and more like a hassle these days. As believers, many of us approach the rainy seasons of life in the same way. It feels less like an adventure and more like an inconvenience. But God has lessons for us to learn and beauty for us to enjoy even during the rainy seasons of life.

The rainy seasons in life are times when there is so much going on that everything feels like a burden or an inconvenience. The rain keeps coming. Perhaps you have more bills than you can afford to pay or kids who always seem to be sick. Days when you feel like you just can't take one more thing. This is the rainy season of life.

The key to seeing the beauty of God in the rainy seasons lies in our perspective. Rainy seasons have the tendency to take away our joy because we're always focused on what we need to do to survive. But as much as rainy seasons can be a burden, they can also be a blessing. Think about the farmer waiting for the rain to water his crops, or the arid desert thirsting for water. As believers we can view the rain as a burden or a blessing. The fact is, as believers we don't really have much to complain about. We are saved and set apart for heaven.

Things go wrong because we live in a fallen world and often, unexpected events and situations can arise. Sometimes it seems like the sun is never out and the rain clouds are all we can see. We must realize that we can praise the Lord no matter what season we are in.

God doesn't cease to be good to you just because you're experiencing a rainy season of rough times in your life. God promises that He is able to work all things—even the hard times—together for the good of those who love Him and are called according to His purpose. He is not trying to discourage you or hurt you by allowing difficulties in your life. He has a purpose! It all has to do with our perspective. Don't let the rain stop you from living radically for the Lord.

One way to alter our perspective during the rainy seasons is to focus on what we know to be true about God and ourselves. We know that God is a fortress we can run to for shelter during the storm. We know God loves us so much that He sent His only Son to die for us. We know that our afflictions are achieving for us something far better! They are achieving for us an eternal glory! That's why we can be thankful even during the hard, rainy seasons of life; God is using these trials to work out His glory in us.

Rainy seasons can also be a sign that there's worse weather up ahead. Sometimes it gets worse before it gets better. Don't let a little rain tempt you away from the Lord. Instead, let the Lord change your perspective to see trials as preparation for future storms. Let these rainy seasons drive you closer to your Redeemer for protection. In the end you'll be thankful for what He did.

# THE RAIN
## QUESTIONS FOR REFLECTION

1. We all carry burdens. According to Jesus, what should we do with our burdens and what will He do?

Read Matthew 11:28-30 to answer this question.

_____

_____

_____

_____

2. According to James, how should we look at our hard times? What are those hard times producing for you?

Read James 1:2-4 to answer this question.

_____

_____

_____

_____

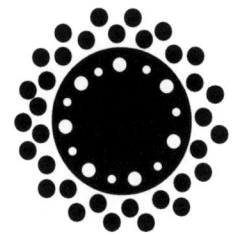

CHAPTER 4

# THE DARKNESS

"But immediately Jesus spoke to them, saying, 'Be of good cheer! It is I; do not be afraid.'"

MATTHEW 14:27

HERE IN MOBILE, ALABAMA, the rain falls so ferociously that cars slow down to a crawl. Visibility is reduced to only a few feet; no one can see anything out of their front windshield. Hazard lights become a necessity during those conditions. Reduced visibility combined with the severe weather can make driving very dangerous. It is not uncommon to see accidents along the side of the road.

Storms in our own lives can also seriously diminish our ability to see clearly. With reduced visibility, we feel like we're driving blind causing us deep anxiety. Our faith is tested as we wonder what God is doing. *How long is this trial going to last? Will I ever survive this? Is my life always going to be like this? Is there any reason to hope now? Why is God allowing me to go through this?* These questions and more race through our minds as we try to make sense of the storm with limited ability to see clearly.

The disciples found themselves in a similar situation when in the middle of the night, they saw Jesus walking toward them on the water—except they didn't know it was Him. It was completely dark out and they were terrified. They couldn't see. During another storm, when the disciples thought their lives were over, Jesus was sleeping peacefully in the boat. The difference between Jesus and His disciples in both moments was this: Jesus was filled with peace while the disciples were filled with fear.

When we lose visibility or our ability to see in the midst of stormy weather, we are often filled with fear. *What's going to happen next? Will I make it through this alive?* But these are the very moments when Jesus asks us to trust Him using our spiritual eyes of faith. The storms help us to build up more faith in Jesus for the future. Jesus called Peter in the midst of the storm, in the darkness of night, to get out of the boat and come to Him. I'm sure that moment changed Peter's life. Sometimes we need storms to impair our physical sight and human understanding so that we can see through the eyes of faith. Storms can peel away the lens of pride that many of us hold on to. They remind us that we cannot live this life without the Lord.

To fear is not our only recourse when caught in the midst of a storm. Jesus told the disciples not to be afraid and He says the same thing to us! How can we have peace in our hearts when we're in a dark place? The answer is—Jesus. He is always with us, even in the storms of life.

Jesus has commanded us not to worry or fear. Why? Because there will not be any more times to be worried or fearful in your life? No—He has commanded us not to be worried or afraid because *He is with us.* We can experience His peace even in the darkest places.

# **THE DARKNESS**
## QUESTIONS FOR REFLECTION

1. When our visibility is limited by the storms in our life, where does God want us to look?

Read Colossians 3:2 to answer this question.

_____

_____

_____

_____


2. What exhortation does God have for us about fear? Why shouldn't we be afraid?

Read Isaiah 41:10 to answer this question. This is a good verse to memorize.

_____

_____

_____

_____

# CHAPTER 5

# THE STORM

"Now when He got into a boat, His disciples followed Him. And suddenly a great tempest arose on the sea, so that the boat was covered with the waves. But He was asleep. Then His disciples came to Him and awoke Him, saying, 'Lord, save us! We are perishing!'"

MATTHEW 8:23-25

YEARS AGO BEFORE WE had any children, my wife and I took a trip to San Francisco. We visited all the usual tourist sites, ate clam chowder from a bowl made of sourdough bread, and drank lots of coffee. The Golden Gate Bridge is arguably the biggest attraction in San Francisco and we didn't want to miss visiting the site. Rather than walking across the bridge as most tourists do, we opted for a boat tour which would not only take us right up to the bridge but give us a unique view of this magnificent attraction. We didn't have much money, so we decided to take the cheapest tour which set sail on a small boat. The boat had no amenities and appeared to have weathered quite a few storms. While she could carry about twenty passengers, on this day there were only a few others brave enough to hop in with us.

We got on the boat wearing our long jackets, beanies and scarves and set out toward the bridge. Right away we noticed that the water was much rougher than we thought. From the shore, the whitecaps looked beautiful and small. But from our new perspective on the boat, the waves were quite large. The farther we got out into the bay, the bigger the waves grew, and I began to worry. The boat began to rock violently as each wave hit and then continued to roll back and forth as it recovered from each wave. Then some water began to come aboard the ship, I was in a panic! It didn't help that the freezing water combined with the harsh wind was chilling us both to the bones. We were shaking, shivering and distressed. Right around that time, the captain decided it was too dangerous to continue and we headed back toward the marina. At that exact moment, a huge wave came overboard smacking me right in the face. I felt defeated. We missed seeing the bridge up close, but in the end we were just happy to be back on land!

Perhaps you have found yourself in a similar situation. You thought the whitecaps looked beautiful, but now that you're out in the midst of the storm all you want to do is get back to shore! When we are in the midst of storms, being tossed back and forth, it is in our nature to want to escape. We want to give up and head back to the shore. We think to ourselves, *If this was God's will, there wouldn't be any hardships or difficulty, so this must not be God's will.* We need to remember that God is sovereign and often allows us to go through storms so that we might learn to depend on Him and Him alone. If we never experienced difficult situations or hard seasons, we wouldn't have the opportunity to see God at work in the midst of our storms.

In the previous chapter, I briefly mentioned one of the times the disciples found themselves in the midst of a storm out at sea. The storm was so great that Matthew calls it a *great tempest* indicating the ferocity of the wind, saying that the boat was covered by the waves. The disciples, most of whom had fished this sea their entire lives, were terrified. Thinking they were about to die, they cried out, "Lord, save us!" Jesus awoke and with a word, calmed the storm and the sea (Matthew 8:23-27).

The disciples had the opportunity to see firsthand the power of God as Jesus calmed the storm. But they only had that incredible opportunity because they were in the midst of the storm. The same is true for you and me. Sometimes the Lord leads us into storms so that we might see Him working in our lives. Other times, the Lord allows us to go through a storm so that we might cry out to Him to save us. In either case, we need to remember that He is in control of the storms and more than able to save us.

I find it interesting that when the disciples cried out to Jesus, He said, "Why are you fearful, O you of little faith?" (Matthew 8:26). This was likely the biggest storm the disciples had ever seen, and yet Jesus rebukes them for being fearful. Why? I believe it is because they were looking at the storm and not at Jesus. When we look around at the storm we find ourselves in, it is easy to feel overwhelmed, afraid or discouraged. Perhaps we've never seen a storm this big, perhaps our circumstances feel unmanageable—like waves threatening to capsize the boat. In those moments, it is easy to look at what's going on around us and be filled with fear. Jesus asks us to use our eyes of faith and look beyond the storm raging all around us.

*"These things I have spoken to you, that in Me you may have peace. In the world you will have tribulation; but be of good cheer, I have overcome the world."*
**—John 16:33**

# THE STORM
## QUESTIONS FOR REFLECTION

1. How did the apostle Paul describe the circumstances he had gone through, and how did he acknowledge God in those trials?

Read 2 Corinthians 4:8-9 to answer this question.

_____

_____

_____

_____

2. In 2 Corinthians 12:7-10, the apostle Paul reveals that he asked the Lord three times to deliver him from an affliction. What reason does the Lord give the apostle Paul for allowing this hardship to remain in his life?

Read 2 Corinthians 12:7-10 to answer this question.

_____

_____

_____

_____

# CHAPTER 6

# THE
# CLOUDS

"They are clouds without water, carried about by the winds; late autumn trees without fruit, dead, pulled up twice by the roots."

JUDE 1:12 b

HANNAH IS MY FIRSTBORN. When she entered the world, she let out a small cry as I cut her umbilical cord and presented her to my wife. Hannah's soft cry filled the room, and I hardly noticed the activity of the nurses around us. My wife and I gazed at each other, tears filling our eyes and joy overflowing our hearts. It was like a scene out of the movies.

When it came time for our second daughter, Lily, to be born, I was expecting something similar. Lily arrived in complete silence. No beautiful baby cry. No gasp of air. Nothing. I was in a panic. Noises filled the room that I hadn't remembered from the first time; nurses scurrying about, instruments being moved around the table, and my wife's breathing. I tried to calm my own emotions and reassure my wife that everything was fine, but I didn't believe it myself. After a few minutes, we finally heard Lily's cry and we both sighed in relief. Lily had swallowed some meconium and it had to be suctioned out. It wasn't an emergency or a reason to panic, but for a few moments I thought it was.

Have you ever been certain there was a storm coming, only to look up and realize the clouds had passed? Or that it wasn't even a storm at all? There have been many times in my life where what I was expecting to happen, did not happen. The clouds came, but the storm, the wind and the rain never did. Sometimes what we see ahead looks threatening, but the storm never comes.

This is why it's so important for us as believers to have our foundation built upon the Rock of Jesus Christ. If we changed our direction or plans every time we saw clouds, we would live in a constant state of uncertainty. As I shared in the first chapter, as we build our foundation on Christ, it is essential that we prepare for the storms of life that will inevitably come. Preparation is vital to the stability of our foundation. But if we are always just preparing for and fretting over cloudy skies, we will never get the real work done.

It has been my experience at times what appears to be a storm is really just Satan, whose purpose is to steal, kill, and destroy (John 10:10), trying to distract us from pursuing the path God has placed before us. It's clouds without rain. We look up and see bad weather and interpret, *God doesn't want us to go that way.* One of Satan's key methods of warfare is distraction. If he can get you off the course God has planned for you, he is winning.

Clouds without rain might look like your employer telling you that there will be layoffs. You weren't told that you were going to lose your job, but those storm clouds are so frightening you get off course and begin worrying about your future. Clouds without rain can take on many different forms, but I primarily see them as distractions that bring on fear or worry.

When we build the foundation of our spiritual home upon Jesus Christ, then we don't have to worry or fear when storm clouds come, whether they are merely threatening rain or truly a tempest of momentous size. Our home is stable and our foundation is secure. Perhaps we will be among the ones to experience the company-wide layoff. We can trust that God is with us and will provide for us because He promises that He will.

The key to not getting distracted with fears or worries about a yet-to-happen storm is to keep our eyes fixed upon Jesus. When clouds threaten to bring storms, we can lift our hands and our hearts to Him and ask Him to lead us safely through.

# THE CLOUDS
## QUESTIONS FOR REFLECTION

1. What is the key to focusing upon the Lord through the storms?

Read Isaiah 26:3 to answer this question.

_____

_____

_____

_____

2. Proverbs 3:5-6 lists three things that will help us stay the course during each season of life. What are the three things we need to do? What will the Lord do?

Read Proverbs 3:5-6 to find the answers.

_____

_____

_____

_____

# CONCLUSION

*"For I am persuaded that neither death nor life, nor angels nor principalities nor powers, nor things present nor things to come, nor height nor depth, nor any other created thing, shall be able to separate us from the love of God which is in Christ Jesus our Lord."* —**Romans 8:38-39**

I know that you, like me, have experienced some difficult times. Storms you never thought you'd experience have rocked your world and left you shaken, or worse. I want to encourage you that God has an amazing way of using the storms we are facing or have endured for our good if we will allow Him (Romans 8:28). Nothing is wasted with God.

I'll never forget when my Mom died of cancer. She had already survived lung cancer, but the cancer came back and overtook her brain. For the last year of her life, my sisters and I took care of her. The chemo had caused hair loss and had left her incredibly thin and weaker with each passing day. One morning when I was with her, she asked me to get her a cup of coffee from the kitchen. Not only was she unable to get up, but that day when I handed her the mug, she could barely hold it and ended up spilling the coffee on herself. She looked at me, and I could see the fight had left her. She began to sob quietly, because she didn't even have the energy left to cry. I was heartbroken.

I rubbed her shoulder and told her that it was going to be OK as I began to wipe up the coffee that had spilled onto her clothing. I said that it was going to be OK, but deep inside I knew that it would never be OK. She was dying. We were not created for death and the grave, but for life and that eternal. It was one of the hardest storms I have ever endured.

Sometime later, I overheard my mom recalling the event to my sisters. "Mike said it was going to be OK," she said with some confidence. I had encouraged her in a moment when she felt defeat. My mom had always been the strong one in our family, but even she needed to be encouraged to trust God and press on with whatever time she had left.

The Bible paints this paradox of life and death very clearly. As believers, we live between these two worlds. Through the sacrifice of Jesus on the cross, we are free from spiritual death; and yet we still see and experience physical death and storms on this earth. Even so, we can also experience abundant spiritual life in this physical world. When the storms rage all around us, we can know God's peace and comfort in the midst. We are going to be OK.

Perhaps you have been through storms that have left you weak, tired, sick, and bruised. Let me encourage you: God is holding the broken pieces of your heart and promises to mend and heal you. He will hold your hand when you feel you're sinking. He reassures you even though you may have fallen again. God loves you and is with you. He cares for you. You are not alone.

Perhaps you have discovered through the storms of life that parts of your foundation were not established upon the Rock of Jesus Christ. When your house was hit by the rains, the wind, and the darkness, it exposed a weakness in the foundation. Don't be discouraged. As you rebuild, look to Jesus, the author and finisher of your faith, to help you build upon the truth of His Word rather than on the shifting sands of this world. Lean on the Lord and let Him guide you and give you the strength you need to make it through the storms you will face.

*"If we are faithless, He remains faithful; He cannot deny Himself."* **—2 Timothy 2:13**

# ABOUT THE AUTHOR

Mike Sternad is the senior pastor of Calvary Chapel Mobile in Mobile, Alabama, a church he planted in September 2017. At the heart of this ministry is a strong focus on teaching the Word of God and sharing it with as many people as possible. Mike believes that he himself is proof of the power of God's Word to transform a lost and broken individual into a blessed man, husband and father. He and his wife, Brianne, have two daughters, Hannah and Lily.

To see more of what Mike has written,
visit www.mikesternad.com or look up Mike Sternad on Amazon.

Made in the
USA
Lexington, KY